CHESTER
in the 1950s
Ten Years that Changed a City

CHESTER
in the 1950s
Ten Years that Changed a City

PAUL HURLEY

AMBERLEY

First published 2014

Amberley Publishing
The Hill, Stroud
Gloucestershire, GL5 4EP

www.amberley-books.com

British Library Cataloguing in Publication Data.
A catalogue record for this book is available from the British Library.

ISBN 978 1 4456 3673 3 (PRINT)
ISBN 978 1 4456 3691 7 (EBOOK)

Typesetting and Origination by Amberley Publishing.
Printed in Great Britain.

Contents

Acknowledgements

This book could not have been compiled without the help of my good friend and respected Chester historian Len Morgan, who allowed me access to his large archive of photographs, history and anecdotes. Len and his wife, Joan, were most welcoming, courteous and helpful. I also benefitted from the assistance given by historian Steve Howe, who allowed me to dip into his excellent series of websites at http://www.chesterwalls.info/. If your interest is Chester history, then this website should be in your list of favourites. I would also like to thank Will Brown for allowing me to use the photograph of the Chester police and the Rowton Hall hotel. Finally, my wife Rose, for her patience during the writing of the book and her attention to detail when proof-reading it.

Author Information

Paul Hurley is a freelance writer, author and a member of the Society of Authors. He has a novel, newspaper and magazine credits and lives in Winsford, Cheshire, with his wife Rose. He has two sons and two daughters.

Contact www.paul-hurley.co.uk

Also by the Same Author

Fiction
Waffen SS Britain

Non-Fiction
Middlewich (with Brian Curzon)
Northwich Through Time
Winsford Through Time
Villages of Mid Cheshire Through Time
Frodsham and Helsby Through Time
Nantwich Through Time
Chester Through Time (with Len Morgan)
Middlewich & Holmes Chapel Through Time
Sandbach, Wheelock & District Through Time
Knutsford Through Time
Macclesfield Through Time
Cheshire Through Time
Northwich, Winsford & Middlewich Through Time

Introduction

The 1950s were an era of change. The lifestyles and aspirations of the 1930s had been brutally brought to an end by the Second World War, and shortages caused by it still existed. The birth rate was high, with the baby boomer generation of children being born to reunited parents, into a world that would never be the same again. The era progressed from the big-band sound to the dawn of the hit parade, when Al Martino had the first number one with 'Here in my Heart' in November 1952. Musical tastes travelled through a decade of sounds to the last number one of the 1950s, which was Emile Ford and the Checkmates with 'What Do You Want To Make Eyes At Me For?' As well as music, people of all ages were different – they dressed differently and acted differently; even their aspirations were different. Nearly all adults smoked, and children playing in the street with their friends were safe. They climbed trees, skinned their knees and ripped their clothes. They made dens in woodland and got into fights, but nobody sued anybody. The pavements were uneven but no one blamed the council if they tripped. Sweets were a treat. Wagon Wheel chocolate bars seemed bigger and people ate politically incorrect things like Black Jacks. Policemen were to be feared – they weren't glorified social workers constantly watching their backs – and children would get a clip round the ear when they had been naughty. To keep them healthy, mums gave them a teaspoon of malt and cod liver oil before school. Beef dripping was in abundance and made great chips!

The ten years from 1950 started off with children being seen and not heard, young boys dressing like their dads and young girls dressing like their mums, to an explosion in youth culture from the mid-1950s onwards. Fashions changed; out went baggy trousers and in came drainpipes and winkle pickers, teddy boys and those whose aspiration involved British motorbikes – the bigger the better. Before you actually reached your goal, you could wear the leathers and go to war with the Teds. Most of it is viewed now with rose-coloured spectacles, the fun times remembered with nostalgia.

A Railway Poster From the 1950s

Nationalisation was brought in by the Labour government from 1945 to 1950, which saw the nationalisation of utilities, the foundation of the NHS, extended National Insurance, British Railways, British Waterways and the independence of India. Britain's involvement in another war in Korea also commenced in 1950, shortly before Churchill returned to power. A Tory government remained as the governing party until 1964. The ownership of cars increased as the decade progressed, but pedal cycles still predominated as an affordable mode of transport, providing opportunities to exercise and burn off the calories – not that anyone considered that much of a benefit at the time. The roads were safer, even if the seat belt-free cars weren't. All the time, the spectre of another war, one that everyone thought would blow up the world, hung over the country. The USSR went from being our friend in the Second World War to being our future enemy in the Cold War, a war that could turn hot with a word out of place by the great and good. This was another reason to enjoy the peace while it lasted, and to hope that our soldiers returned safely from Korea, Malaya and, later, Suez. In July 1957, Prime Minister Harold Macmillan told the nation that they had 'never had it so good', while summing up the fragile prosperity of the 1950s and warning of the dangers of inflation. Not much change there then.

Eastgate Street, 1950s

But what of the Cheshire city of Chester? Chester is an ancient city that now boasts almost intact city walls. Several towns and cities in England were walled to keep out invaders and to protect those that the invaders had successfully taken over. Some are still to be found in various stages of fragmentary remains, excavation and rebuilding. Chester and York are the only two cities left with a virtually intact perimeter wall. Chester's walls date from Roman times, with much demolition and rebuilding in between. They protected the city from the Welsh and then again during the Civil War, when they were damaged in the fighting. They provided a grandstand on 24 September 1645 for King Charles I to stand in the Phoenix tower and view the battle of Rowton Heath, an assault that saw his cavalry and foot soldiers well and truly beaten. Modern traffic and transport demanded a route through or around the city. Fortunately, with a few glaring errors, the planners allowed this to occur with as little damage as possible, although, inevitably, there had to be some. In the 1800s, the railway had to be given a route through the city walls and several city gates had to be widened or altered to allow the passage of more than just horse and cart. The walls stayed in place. It is now possible to take a pleasant stroll around the city with just a few very slight deviations from the walls proper. During this stroll you may gaze down at the ancient amphitheatre, the largest of its kind uncovered in Great Britain. You will pass the famous cathedral and then enter back into the old city, where alterations have occasionally been made. In the main, these have been done sympathetically and in keeping with the general antiquity of the surrounding buildings. You can see why this city is one of the most visited in Britain.

City Walls at Bridgegate

Along came the Second World War, that destructive episode in the infrastructure of Britain, when many of the cities were bombed to destruction. Coventry was the most notable example, but Liverpool, London and many others saw their vistas change and their ancient buildings turned to rubble. In 1942, the RAF bombed the ancient German cities of Lübeck and Rostock and an angry German hierarchy instigated what were called the Baedeker Raids. These used the German Baedeker tourist guides, which highlighted Britain's ancient towns and cities, and from these, militarily unimportant and picturesque places were targeted. Canterbury, Exeter, Bath, Norwich and York were subjected to these vindictive bombing raids. Chester somehow escaped the attentions of the Luftwaffe, perhaps because planes were being lost for little military gain and Rommel's fortunes had changed in the desert. Either way, the fortunes of war had turned in Chester's favour.

Bridge Street, 1950

Whatever the reason, Chester was left almost bomb-free, despite the fact that it housed important war industries, such as Vickers-Armstrong. This had its aircraft factory at Broughton and also went by the name of Hawarden Airport. During the war, they built 5,786 Wellington bombers in the Broughton factory and, with a massive RAF airbase at Sealand, there had to be some action. There was a succession of air raids from late 1940 to early 1941, but these did little damage. During the war, there were 232 alerts: forty-four high-explosive bombs and three incendiaries were dropped on the city and, in the process, three people were killed and three seriously injured. This meant that, while other cities were rebuilding from the rubble of their air raids, Chester was virtually unscathed, but what was it like in Chester after the Second World War? What was Chester like in the 1950s?

On the Dee

After the war, Chester's prosperity more or less continued from how it had been pre-war. There were still some old, established manufacturing concerns like the two tobacco companies, the largest of these being Messrs Thomas Nicholls & Co., manufacturers of tobacco and snuff products. The company was established in Chester during the 1780s, and the attractive red-brick buildings stood directly opposite the Groves and Bandstand on the other side of the river.

Chester Business

The Old Snuff Works

These attractive buildings, belonging to T. Nichols & Co., were closed in the late 1950s and allowed to stand empty. In the 1960s, there was a fire and the buildings were entirely demolished. As already mentioned, there were some blips in the excellent redevelopment of the city over the years, and here one such blip was allowed. The beautiful red-brick 'snuff works', as it was called locally, was replaced by the exceedingly ugly Salmon Leap flats, which resemble egg boxes. To enhance their ugliness they were even painted pink. At least now they have been painted cream. They were built at the Old Dee Bridge end of the Nichols site, giving the tourists an unpleasant change of vista from the ancient city walls. The beautiful buildings were in the care of Messrs John Douglas, Parkes & Penton, and other noted architects who transformed the city over the years to what we see today. Nowadays, the factory would probably be converted into apartments and the view across the ancient bridge and the wild River Dee tumbling over the weir would be a little more picturesque. The rest of the Nichols site was landscaped and a footpath to the meadows constructed. At the far end, the Salmon Leap itself survives, and the waterwheel, which once powered Nicholls' snuff mill, has been restored.

Salmon Leap Flats, 2014

These industries had been joined by the newer, larger, and more modernised enterprises such as Brookhirst Electrical Switchgear, and two makers of metal window frames. One of these, Williams Bros, began around 1859 as a timber business in the Kaleyards, but later switched to making metal windows and relocated to Victoria Road. The firm of Williams & Williams was founded in 1910, and also made metal window frames at premises in the old engineering works on the corner of Victoria Road and George Street. It later became a company of national significance called W. G. Kaleyards Metal Windows Ltd, of Victoria Road, a company that lasted until 1976 when the receivers were called in.

W. G. Kaleyards Ltd

Chester, in 1955, had some 2,000 railwaymen. (*See Chester and its Railways.*) There were also 1,000 employees at Crosville Motor Services, the regional bus company based in Chester. In the photograph overleaf of Northgate Street in 1958, along with the image above, typical Crosville buses can be seen.

Opposite above: Old Northgate Street from the Northgate, 1958

Crosville is a company that originated in Chester, so is worthy of a mention in the lead up to the 1950s. Motor manufacturing in Chester consisted of a few cars made by George Crosland-Taylor and his French associate Georges de Ville between 1906 and 1910, using parts imported from France. Five cars were produced bearing the Crosville name, but only two were built in Chester. From 1910, the firm concentrated on running buses. The company was formed as Crosville Motor Company Ltd on 27 October 1906. Its intention was to build motor cars. The company name was an amalgamation of 'Crosland' and 'de Ville'.

In 1909, Crosville started its first bus service between Chester and Ellesmere Port, and by 1929 they had consolidated an operating area covering the Wirral and parts of Lancashire, Cheshire and Flintshire. In 1928, the Railways (Road Transport) Act had come into force. This gave the four railway companies the opportunity to provide bus services. However, rather than run in competition, they bought into or purchased outright existing bus companies in the same way as they had taken over some of the canals. In February 1929, the LMS (London, Midland & Scottish Railway) made an offer of £400,000 to purchase Crosville, which was completed in November 1929. The new LMS (Crosville) company also purchased Holyhead Motors and UNU Motor Services of Caernarvon in the next few months.

Not long after this, the four railway companies reached an agreement with the Tilling & British Automobile Traction (T&BAT) to complete a cross-holding deal, whereby each organisation held a 50 per cent share in a series of jointly held and consolidated regional bus companies. LMS (Crosville) was therefore merged with T&BAT's Royal Blue of Llandudno and, on 15 May 1930, renamed the new company Crosville Motor Services Ltd after only nine months of LMS ownership. In the next few months, the company consolidated its majority share of the North Wales coastal services, buying up various smaller private companies that operated in the Crosville area, including White Rose Motor Services of Rhyl, Red Dragon of Denbigh, Burton of Tarporley, North Wales Silver Motors and Llangoed Red Motors. On 1 May 1933, the Great Western Railways northern Welsh service, Western Transport, was amalgamated with Crosville.

During the Second World War, Crosville had gone from strength to strength to meet the needs of wartime. One instance was the Royal Ordnance Factory near Wrexham, with its 30,000 workers needing 200 buses a day.

In 1942, Crosville became a subsidiary of the Tilling group and their colour scheme was changed from maroon to green as they continued to prosper. By 1950, however, the post-war boom had begun to subside and prices rapidly spiralled. Fare increases were introduced in an effort to maintain services, but this only led to a fall in passenger numbers and further increases in fares, a situation that was to be continually repeated over the next forty years. Throughout the 1950s, Crosville suffered (as did most bus companies) from a serious staff shortage. During this period, employees in the bus industry were poorly paid and, accordingly, recruitment was difficult. One-man operation was seen as one of the options needed to make effective use of the labour force, but union opposition forced the company to delay plans to introduce it throughout the network and affected its viability. It wasn't until the middle of the next decade that one-man operation was introduced company-wide, and clippies became a thing of the past.

Opposite below: William Vernon & Son, 1950s

Another ancient Chester company was William Vernon & Sons, of Nos 47 to 57 Northgate Street. In this photograph, we can see the company premises during the 1950s, but the history of the company goes way back. During the early 1800s, the suburbs of Chester were being extended and the most notable builders of the age were William Boden, Thomas Edwards and, of course, William Vernon. In the early days of the railways, William Vernon & Son were a big enough company to have their own railway wagons, bearing the William Vernon & Sons logo.

Brookhirst Ltd Staff, Early 1950s

Another famous Chester company was Brookhirst & Co., which was started in 1898 with a staff of twelve by John A. Hirst, a pioneer in electrical invention and development. His partner in the firm was Percy Shelley Brook (Brook-Hirst). The firm's original works were in Victoria Road, later moving to George Street and subsequently to Newry Park in East Chester. Owing to the inspiration of John Hirst, the firm was at the forefront of technical development in the switchgear industry during its early years. By 1908, the firm had expanded and modern works were built at Newry Park in East Chester with two parts: one for the manufacture of direct-current control gear, and the other for the manufacture of alternating-current control gear, along with a range of small power control gear for motors up to about 10 hp. By the 1920s, major orders from abroad were being received, especially from foreign navies. In 1943, metal industries acquired Electrical Switchgear & Associated Manufacturers Ltd, which owned Brookhirst Switchgear Ltd. The company continued giving work to a lot of Chester citizens, shown here in a photograph of some of the staff at the company in the early 1950s.

In 1960, metal industries integrated its long-established subsidiaries, Brookhirst Switchgear Ltd and Igranic Electric Co. Ltd, into Brookhirst Igranic Ltd. In the late 1960s, the Northgate works in Newry Park were closed, but production continued at Bedford and the name Brookhirst Igranic Ltd was used until the firm became part of Cutler Hammer Europa.

Assay Office, No. 13 Goss Street, 1957

The last years of the famous Chester Assay Office were the 1950s. Silversmith activity in Chester began in AD 925, but it has only been well documented since 1225. Until the end of the seventeenth century, hallmarking was not regular, although a guild of silversmiths was appointed to survey the silver standard. Chester was not one of the towns allowed to open new Assay offices under the Act of Henry VI in 1423, but hallmarking activity in Chester was already established.

Here are the descriptions of the Chester hallmarks during the years of operation:
1686 – 1701: Three wheatsheaves ('garbs') with sword.
1701 – 1779: Three wheatsheaves/three lions halved.
1779 – 1961: Three wheatsheaves with sword.

Silver hallmarked in Chester and actually from the city is very rare, as no silversmiths were operating in the town after 1820–30. However, the abundance of Chester hallmarks on silverware dating from around 1880 to 1930 is due to the fact that silver crafted in Birmingham, or by local silversmiths operating in Liverpool and Manchester, was sent for hallmarking to the Chester Assay office. The Chester Assay office closed down in 1962.

Chester Telephone Exchange, 1950s

In 1951, 1,000 post office and telecommunications workers were employed locally. In 1898, there were 168 subscribers to Chester's telephone service, and most of them were businesses. Operated by the Liverpool and Manchester Exchange Telephone Co., as a subsidiary of the United Telephone Co. under Post Office licence, the UTC merged with its subsidiaries as the National Telephone Co. in 1891. Its Chester Exchange and regional head office were in Godstall Chambers, St Werburgh Street. The exchange was transferred to a new building next to the main post office in St John Street in 1908, in anticipation of the Post Office's acquisition of the telephone system, which took effect in 1912. It moved again in 1950 to a neo-Georgian building on the north side of Little John Street, which was built for the purpose in 1939.

Off the Wall Pub, 2014

When automation arrived, the need for a fully-manned telephone exchange, as in the first photograph, diminished and the building was sold off, becoming a public house called Off The Wall. A false floor has split the once high building into two floors. The ground floor can be seen in the modern photograph.

Chester and the Armed Forces

Cheshire Regiment, 1954

The Army has always had a close connection with the city. The castle was the home of the Cheshire Regiment from 1881, and it remained there until 1940, when a depot was established at the Dale Barracks on the edge of the city. In the 1950s, the Cheshire Regimental Headquarters was moved back to the castle, where they remained until amalgamation into the Mercian Regiment in 2007. During the 1950s, the Cheshire Regiment found themselves serving in Cyprus from 1951 to 1954. The Greek Cypriot organisation Eoka attacked and killed British soldiers on and off duty. The photograph shows a march through the city in 1958.

Cheshire Regiment Marching up Bridge Street to the Town Hall, 1958

Always at the forefront of action around the world, the old Cheshire Regiment's real home was Chester. It was from here that they left to participate in the dispute over the Suez Canal in the 1950s. Not the most glorious of actions taken by Britain, but that was in no way the fault of our brave fighting men.

Hodgsons Camp Suez, 1954

Cheshire Regiment Returning from Suez Aboard *Empire Fowey*, 1954

The headquarters of the Army's Western Command was in Chester. The Command was established in 1905, and was originally called the Welsh & Midland Command before changing its name in 1906. In 1907, Western Command relocated to Watergate House in Chester. In 1938, after a brief stay in temporary accommodation at Broughton, it moved to a new purpose-built neo-Georgian property at Queen's Park in Chester. It covered Wales and the counties of Cumberland, Westmoreland, Lancashire, Staffordshire, Shropshire, Herefordshire, Cheshire and Gloucestershire, as well as the Isle of Man and the coastal defence garrisons of Berehaven, Queenstown and Lough Swilly. When the Army left, the building was upgraded to serve as the headquarters of the Capital Bank.

Royal Visits

Old Eaton Hall, 1900

The title Duke of Westminster was created by Queen Victoria in 1874, and the current holder is Gerald Grosvenor, 6th Duke of Westminster, who is godfather to the young Prince George of Cambridge. The Duke's family home is Eaton Hall in Chester and his family's noble title can be traced back to Richard Grosvenor, who was created Baronet of Eaton in January 1622. Sir Richard Grosvenor, the 7th Baronet, was created Baron Grosvenor in 1761 and, in 1784, became both Viscount Belgrave and Earl Grosvenor under George III. The title of Marquis of Westminster was bestowed upon Robert Grosvenor, the 2nd Earl Grosvenor, at the coronation of William IV in 1831.

Beginning in 1863, the training hulks *Britannia* and *Hindostan* were used to train officers for the Royal Navy, and the present Britannia Royal Naval College buildings date from 1905. The bombing of the college in September 1942 forced a change in training policy, and both staff and students were evacuated to Eaton Hall until the end of the war. It became known as HMS *Britannia* or Royal Naval College Eaton Hall, Chester, and future officers were trained there until 1946. After 1946, the Army moved in.

National Service continued after the war and hundreds of officers were needed for the Army. Lt-Gen. Sir Brian Horrocks, who commanded Western Command in Chester, recognised the potential of the then vacant estate of the Duke of Westminster. With the Duke's agreement, he moved in the 164 Officer Cadet Training Unit to Eaton Hall. It primarily trained officers for the infantry, though other corps were also trained there, notably for the Royal Electrical and Mechanical Engineers (REME). Some 15,000 officer cadets were trained there between 1946 and 1958 when, due to the phasing out of National Service, it was merged with the Cavalry Officer Cadet School at Mons Barracks, Aldershot.

Like most large houses occupied by the services during the war, the fabric of Eaton Hall suffered to such an extent that it was decided it would be demolished and rebuilt. Initially this rebuild, which included a flat roof and a rather unappealing aspect, left a little to be desired. After a slight rebuild and the addition of another level with a hipped roof, it once again looked the part, as can be seen from this more modern photograph.

New Eaton Hall

In 1951, Princess Elizabeth visited Eaton Hall and passed through Chester. In the first photograph, the Queen's motorcade travels through the crowds of well-wishers in Chester, and in the second, she can be seen walking with Lord Leverhulme as the scouts stand smartly to attention. Lord Leverhulme was, at the time, the Lord Lieutenant of Cheshire, and the Queen was visiting The Duke of Westminster at Eaton Hall. The following year, Elizabeth would be crowned Queen.

Royal Visit, April 1951

This was not the only royal visit to Chester. In 1957, the young Queen Elizabeth visited Chester with her husband Prince Philip.

Chester County Hall

As previously mentioned, Her Majesty came to Chester in 1957 and performed a number of duties, visiting patients in Chester Royal Infirmary and presenting colours to troops at Chester Racecourse. Another reason for the visit was to open the new county hall, which was to be the administrative headquarters of the then Cheshire County Council. The county council was formed in 1888 and, since then, had used offices within Chester Castle. By the 1930s, it was decided that more room was required, and so the then county architect, E. Mainwaring Parkes, was tasked with designing a state-of-the-art council building. A neo-Georgian county hall was planned and work began on it in 1938. It occupied the site of the old Chester gaol and work had to stop at the outbreak of the war, not resuming until 1947. Building continued through the 1950s, and by 1957 the building was fit for purpose. Queen Elizabeth visited Chester on 11 July in order to formally open it for business. When asked to comment upon the architecture, the acclaimed architectural historian Nicholas Pevsner noted that, 'It was not an ornament to the riverside view.' Unfortunately, he was not around to comment upon the Salmon Leap flats opposite. The hall was sold to Chester University at the start of the new millennium, and the offices moved in 2009 to the building that replaced the police headquarters, known as the HQ building. It houses the council offices and the Abode Hotel.

Chester Industry

Businesses such as catering, hotels and garages employed 2,000 people in the 1950s. Banking was then (as now) an important industry in the city, with over 3,000 employees. From the post-war days of the 1950s, opportunities for employment in Chester continued to grow. In 1971, there were 1,000 more jobs in banks, insurance companies and other financial services than in 1951. In relation to education, medicine, the law, and other professions, all areas of employment had more than doubled in size to 4,500, again more in 1971 than 1951. The post office had 400 more employees in 1971 than in 1951; the regional electricity board, Manweb, nearly 1,000 more; and local and central government ,an additional 1,400. In financial services, the most notable success was the rise of North West Securities to become a leading finance house. The company was established in Chester in 1948 as a subsidiary of a Colwyn Bay motor dealership, set up to provide loans for buying cars. Expansion and diversification into industrial loans accelerated after it was bought by the Bank of Scotland in 1958.

A small new head office opened in Newgate Street in 1956 and was replaced by a large eight-story building in City Road in 1963 (at the time the largest commercial building in Chester). The company took over other companies and established branches nationwide. The Bank of Scotland is still in Chester in the City Road office block. Although many city-centre workers lived in the suburbs outside the borough boundary, a great deal of labour was provided for industry from the wider region in aircraft, including manufacturing at Broughton, at the Shotton steelworks and in the chemical industry, mostly at Ellesmere Port. The aircraft production at Broughton, which is still a thriving industry today, was even more important during and after the war.

The current Airbus Broughton site was founded in 1939 as a shadow factory for the production of the Vickers Wellington and the Avro Lancaster. After the war, De Havilland took over the factory and it was used to produce various aircraft. Short Brothers, better known as Shorts, was a large aircraft manufacturer responsible for many wartime aircraft. In 1936, the Air Ministry opened a large aircraft plant in Belfast, and Shorts became Short & Harland Ltd., jointly owned by Harland & Wolf and Shorts. After the war, the rest of Shorts' wartime factories had been closed and operations were concentrated in Belfast. In 1948, the company offices followed, and Shorts became a Belfast company in its entirety. In the meantime, in 1947, the De Havilland DH 106 Comet was the first production commercial jetliner. It was a very attractive and modernistic airliner but, being the first of its kind, it suffered with gremlins. Developed and manufactured by De Havilland, at its Hatfield headquarters in Hertfordshire, the Comet 1 prototype first flew on 27 July 1949. It featured an aerodynamically clean design with four De Havilland Ghost turbojet engines buried in the wings, with a pressurised fuselage, and large square windows. For the era, it offered a relatively quiet, comfortable passenger cabin and showed signs of being a commercial success at its 1952 debut. A year after entering commercial service, the Comets began suffering problems, with three of them breaking up during mid-flight in well-publicised accidents. This was later found to be due to catastrophic metal fatigue in the airframes, which was not well understood at the time.

By now, Short & Harland had started to manufacture the aircraft in conjunction with De Havilland, mainly due to the order book being full. As a result of the crashes, the Comet was withdrawn from service and extensively tested to discover the cause; the first incident had been incorrectly blamed on adverse weather. Design flaws, including dangerous stresses at the corners of the square windows and installation methodology, were ultimately identified. As a result, the Comet was extensively redesigned with oval windows, structural reinforcement and other changes. Rival manufacturers meanwhile heeded the lessons learned from the Comet while developing their own aircraft.

A Comet Airliner Travels to Chester by Road

The Comet was also produced at the Broughton factory and, during these tests, it became necessary to convey two of the Comet Mark 2 aircraft from Short & Harland Ltd in Belfast to De Havilland's Broughton site, the journey taking from Saturday 22 October to Tuesday 1 November 1955. Fortunately, we can follow the route of one of them using photographs. Remember, this was before the motorways and the A55, so, accordingly, this huge aircraft had to be towed through the streets of Manchester, Stockport and Chester on its journey from Preston Docks.

Comet Being Loaded

Here we see a photograph of the aircraft being loaded on to the MV Empire Cymric for its voyage across the Irish Sea to Preston Docks.

Comet Going Aboard

All safely stowed, the ship's crew pose for a photograph with their strange cargo.

Empire Cymric Ship's Company

After a safe and uneventful sea voyage from Belfast, the ship arrives at Preston Docks and is carefully unloaded and placed in the capable hands of Pickford's heavy haulage and the powerful Scammel tractor unit.

Comet Being Unloaded

Now the fun bit. The Comet, safely strapped to its quite basic trailer, sets off through the towns and cities of the North West. In 1955, there were no luxuries like multi-wheeled trailers with the steering capability at the rear, but just a simple, old-fashioned draw bar.

Comet Sets Off

From Preston, the convoy enters Manchester and passes Kemsley House, the home of Kemsley Newspapers, owned by Welshman Gomer Berry, 1st Viscount Kemsley and publisher of the *Sunday Times*, the *Daily Sketch* and the *Daily Graphic*. The building is now known as the printworks. It makes for a good period and atmospheric photograph.

Passing Kemsley House, Manchester

The convoy continues to creep carefully through Manchester and Stockport, past the Manchester & Salford Co-operative Society. Members of the team use a pole to lift a telephone wire out of the way. Even the Wolseley police car is polished up for the occasion.

The Comet Still Creeping through Manchester
Eventually, after overnight stops and refreshment breaks, it reaches the tightly packed street of Chester.

The Comet through Chester
Arriving at The Cross, it peeps around the corner to see if the way is clear before proceeding down the usually busy Bridge Street.

The Comet through Chester

Manoeuvring carefully to prevent the demolition of the ancient Rows, the Comet travels down Bridge Street.

The Comet through Chester

At last the convoy arrives at Broughton and is met with congratulations all round for a difficult job well done.

5

Chester Salmon Fishermen

Handbridge Salmon Fishermen, 1958

The River Dee has, for a long time, been one of the better-known salmon rivers in the country. The important reaches for salmon angling are the Dee and its tributaries upstream of Bangor-on-Dee. A limited number of salmon fishermen operate in the estuary and the canalised reach of the river, where the estuary is also the source. In this 1958 photograph, we see two salmon fishermen and a younger boy wielding a hand drill as he works on the boats.

The salmon fishing community lived in Greenway Street and the courts surrounding it in Handbridge, across the Dee from Chester. They all had their own jealously guarded named spots from which to fish, such as Marshead, Lane End, Under the Hills, Crane and Littlewood. Once there were fourteen such places within 2 miles of the Old Dee Bridge. Today there are six. The area of Greenway Street has been redeveloped. Also in the area was Taylor's boatyard, a company that made canal craft and boats, including those for the salmon fishermen. Salmon fishing was a long established occupation in Handbridge that lasted into the 1960s, so let us now have a look at some of the personalities involved in this trade.

Group of Salmon Fishermen, 1950

Here we see a typical group of fishermen photographed in 1950. *From left to right*: Arthur Seddle; John 'Snowy' Buckley, who was also a Saltney Ferryman; Gordon 'Cobbler' Buckley; John Buckley, 'Snowy's' son; Elija 'Bonco' Buckley and Jack Buckley. There follows a photograph of Willy Gerard and Henry Sconce on their salmon boat.

Salmon Fishermen Repairing Nets, Late 1950s
The fishermen drove wooden posts known as stakes into the ground and used them to dry their nets. The final photograph is of salmon fishermen repairing their nets on the river with Grosvenor Bridge in the background in the late 1950s.

Chester Lead Works

Another Chester company was the Chester Lead Works, which incorporated the Chester Shot Tower (also known as the Boughton Shot Tower). It is a Grade II listed shot tower located in the Boughton district, and the tower stands beside the Shropshire Union Canal and forms part of the Chester lead works. Built by Walkers, Parker & Co. in 1799, the tower is the oldest of three remaining shot towers in the UK, and probably the oldest such structure still standing in the world. The circular red-brick tower is 168 feet tall and 30 feet in diameter at the base, tapering to 20 feet at the top. The interior had a spiral staircase and melting pots. The tower was one of the earliest built to manufacture lead shot using the method pioneered in the 1780s by the Bristol inventor William Watts. Molten lead was poured through a pierced copper plate or sieve at the top of the tower, with the droplets forming perfect spheres by surface tension during the fall. The spherical drops were then cooled in a vat of water at the base. Watts' process was less labour intensive than the earlier method of casting shot in moulds. An early use of the tower was to make lead shot for muskets in the Napoleonic Wars, although other methods were developed to manufacture shot during the twentieth century. The Chester tower was still in use as late as 2001.

Lead Works & Canal, 2002
Lead is believed to have been exported at the port of Chester from lead mines in North Wales since the Roman period. The construction of the Chester Canal in the 1770s led to industrial development to the east of Chester, with Walkers, Parker & Co. lead works being established there in the late eighteenth century. The lead industry became one of Chester's major industries during the nineteenth century. It remained in use until 2001, when it closed. The photograph, taken a year after it closed in 2002, is more modern, but shows the lead works as it looked during the 1950s when it was still moulding lead. Although shot towers were very common during the nineteenth century across the country, the Chester tower is the only surviving example that dates from this period.

6

Post-War Plans for Chester

We have looked at some of Chester's industry that existed in the 1950s – a royal visit, aircraft in Bridge Street, fishing on the Dee and Chester's important lead industry. Now let's have a look at post-war plans for the city. As previously mentioned, Chester did not suffer war damage to the same extent as other cities, but modernisation was overdue and would have to be considered. The city's engineer, Charles Greenwood, put forward a Plan for Redevelopment in 1945, which had quite an influence on future development. Chester had some old and overcrowded housing stock and areas of small and outworn houses.

Overleigh Road, Handbridge, 1952
As was the case with towns and cities that really did need a plan to recover from the ravages of war, Chester did it anyway with some bold forward planning. Well, 'bold plans' to some, and perhaps a bit of vandalism to others. The first plan was for an outer and inner ring bypass. The outer was to divert through traffic, with the inner taking local traffic around the shopping centre. Another priority was to remove old and worn-out housing stock, mainly in the Boughton and Newtown areas. This would allow for large-scale planning, with the displaced residents would be rehoused out of the city. The aforementioned Greenway Street, home to the salmon fishermen, would be redeveloped.

Greenway Street, Handbridge, 1954

Also in Handbridge, old terraced houses were demolished in order to build new housing stock for the Grosvenor Estate. The architectural treatment of new buildings within the city walls was to be in fitting with the spirit and character of the area. The inharmonious style of buildings was to be opposed. Outside the walls it was a different matter, and modern buildings would be permitted.

In 1931, the building of the large Lache estate began, and was stopped for the duration of the Second World War, recommencing when hostilities ended. Smaller estates were built, such as the Newton Hall estate between 1957 and 1960, but the big daddy of the post-war Chester council estates was Blacon. By the 1970s, it had become the biggest council estate in Europe. Blacon was originally known as Blakon Hill and was owned by the Marquis of Crewe. The Parish of Blacon (cum Crabwall) was formed in 1923, and on 1 April 1936 most of the parish was transferred to Chester County Borough under the Cheshire County Review Order, 1936. Blacon had been a small farming village community until major building work by Chester City Council began in the early 1950s. The Army had a camp in South Blacon, from just before to just after the Second World War. A mixture of wooden and Nissen huts were occupied by soldiers until the late 1950s. This part of Blacon is referred to as 'the Camp' by local residents. Most of the older and original council estate was built in the ten years up to 1960. 'The Parade' shops, built in 1954 in north Blacon, are a typical example of a Chester city council building. The original plan for the Blacon Estate was for approximately 600 houses, twenty-four shops and a community centre, and the building continued into the next decade. Blacon once had a railway station that was closed during the later Beeching cuts, despite being very busy. The line through is now a pleasant country walk.

Bridge Street, 1955

By the 1950s, there was also acute traffic congestion in the heart of the city and, without some drastic alterations, this could only get worse. Bridge Street was an example of this, as can be seen in this 1955 view of Bridge Street. Grosvenor Street, at the junction with Whitefriars, can also be seen, with two police officers trying to regulate the traffic. The Kings Head hotel on the far left, and most of the buildings, have now gone. Another main street in Chester was Grosvenor Street (*see below*).

The Roodee, 1950s

Chester Racecourse, known as the Roodee, is, according to official records, the oldest racecourse still in use in England. Horse racing at Chester dates back to the early sixteenth century. It is also thought to be the smallest racecourse of significance in England, at 1 mile and 1 furlong long. The 65-acre racecourse is on the banks of the River Dee, and was once a harbour during the Roman settlement of the city. It remained so for some years, the Watergate once leading to the harbour. When the Roodee was a harbour, goods would be taken through the Watergate to a customs house in Watergate Street. As the years passed, the River Dee silted up and became too shallow for larger ships, thus making navigation impossible, and the port was closed. Towards the centre of the field, there is a raised mound with a sandstone plinth that is decorated by a small cross known as a 'rood'. It is from this that the racecourse derives the name 'Roodee'. Roodee is a corruption of 'Rood Eye', meaning the Island of the Cross. According to ancient legend, this cross marks the burial site of a statue of the Virgin Mary that was sentenced to hang after causing the death of Lady Trawst, the wife of the Governor of Hawarden Castle *c.* AD 804. The story purports that Lady Trawst had gone to church to pray for rain, but when her prayers were answered by a tremendous thunderstorm, the statue set in the wall was loosened and fell. It landed on the noble lady, killing her. As a holy object, hanging or burning the statue would be sacrilege, so the statue was left by the banks of the river and miraculously the tide carried it down to Chester. A jury of twelve men tried the statue and found it guilty. If the legend is true, then this is the first recorded case of a jury being used in a court. In an alternative version of the legend, the statue was instead carried to St John's church in Chester. An ancient statue of the Virgin was recorded at the time of the reformation, but may not be the same one, as much damage was done to the ancient church and the statue, with others being smashed down and burned as a relics of popery. The site was formerly the home of the original Chester Midsummer Watch Parade, which was temporarily banned by Oliver Cromwell and finally abolished in 1677. To the east, the racecourse abuts directly onto Chester's ancient city walls, which were once used to moor Roman trading vessels before the course of the river changed. Spectators can still watch races for free from the walls, which offer a clear view of the whole circuit. The Grosvenor Bridge passes over the south-eastern corner of the Roodee.

Grosvenor Bridge

The Grosvenor Bridge is a single-span, stone-arch road bridge crossing the River Dee that carries Grosvenor Road over the river. It was designed by Thomas Harrison and opened by Princess Victoria of Saxe-Coburg-Saalfeld, soon to become Queen Victoria on 17 October 1832. At the time of its construction, the bridge was the longest single-span arch bridge in the world, a title that it retained for thirty years, and it is designated by English Heritage as a Grade I listed building.

At the beginning of the nineteenth century, Chester only had one river crossing, a narrow medieval bridge at Handbridge, the Old Dee Bridge. Heavily congested, it delayed movement through the town. Building a new bridge was prohibitively expensive until Thomas Telford proposed a new road between Shrewsbury and the Irish ferries at Holyhead to facilitate trade between the two islands. The route would have bypassed Chester, greatly reducing the potential income from the lucrative Irish trade routes. A committee was appointed to consider plans for a new bridge, to quicken movement across the city and encourage traders to continue to stop there. At the time, Chester was a major shipbuilding city, and a very tall bridge was required to allow ships to pass underneath. A design by the architect, Thomas Harrison, featuring an arch 60 feet high and 200 feet wide, was chosen. When constructed, it would be the largest arch in the world, described by the chief builder, James Trubshaw, as 'a lasting monument to the glory and superiority of Great Britain'. The arch is of limestone from Anglesey, and the rest the bridge is gritstone. Its span remains the longest masonry arch in Britain.

Original plans called for a bridge between Chester Castle and Wrexham Road. Harrison, however, was concerned that the soft ground there would not support heavy piers. Telford found a drier area downstream and construction was moved there. The first stone was laid by the Marquess of Westminster on 1 October 1827. Construction was finally completed in November 1833, and a toll imposed to pay the £50,000 (roughly £4,020,000 in 2014) construction costs, a large sum at the time. The toll proved harmful to trade and was abolished in 1885, when maintenance was transferred to the Chester Corporation. Harrison died two years into construction – his pupil, William Cole, completed the job. The north of the Roodee course is bordered by a long railway bridge carrying the North Wales Coast Line over the River Dee. The course is overlooked from the opposite bank of the river by the houses of Curzon Park, which can be seen dominating the skyline from any of the three grandstands. In 1539, horse racing was brought to the Roodee. The first recorded race was held on 9 February 1539, though this date is disputed by some. The Mayor of Chester at the time was Mr Henry Gee, whose name led to the use of the term 'gee-gee' for horses. Races originally took place on Shrove Tuesday until 1609, and thereafter on St George's Day, both major festivals during the Middle Ages. Victors were awarded the 'Chester Bells', a set of decorative bells for decorating the horse's bridle and, from 1744, the 'Grosvenor Gold Cup', a small tumbler made from solid gold (later silver). In 1745, the meeting was extended to four days, with one race on each day. In 1766, a May Festival was introduced and, in 1824, the Tradesmen's Cup Race (the predecessor to the Chester Cup) was also introduced.

Chester Race Track

The racecourse was, at this point, still just an open field, with the first grandstand finished in 1817 and the first admittance fee taken in 1897. The stand was rebuilt in 1899/1900, and was later replaced. During the 1950s, the Roodee was the venue for military parades and the Cheshire Show. A military tattoo took place on the field in 1949, giving the city surveyor some work, and a meeting was held to decide on its fate. It consisted of the city surveyor, the park superintendent, the Roodee keeper and the firm of Weston Brothers. It was decided to get a repair quote for the turf, and the Weston Brothers submitted one of £399 to disc harrow approximately 10 acres of land and dress it with sandy soil and reseed. The consequence of this was that the football pitches on the field could not be used, and a Mr Fishwick could not keep his sheep there until the ground had recovered. The Territorial Army and Air Forces Association, whose tattoo it was, were ordered to pay for this work. Throughout the 1950s, the Roodee was the venue for the Cheshire County Show, which was even more popular then than it is today. As a child, it was always an exciting annual trip with school to see the animals close up, enjoying unlimited free samples of pies, cheese and other goodies. This would be followed by attempts to eat our packed lunch and drink our Tizer on the banks overlooking the course.

7

Employment and the Famous Chester Clock

The Chester Clock, 1959

The Eastgate clock stands prominently on the top of the Eastgate into the walled city. It was designed by the Sandiway architect John Douglas to celebrate Queen Victoria's Diamond Jubilee. It was then built by the cousin of John Douglas, James Swindley of Handbridge, with the clock itself provided by J. B. Joyce of Whitchurch. During the 1950s, it had to be wound by hand every week, and is said to be the most photographed clock in the world after Big Ben. By the early 1950s, the clock was in need of repair. The council had received a quote from the original manufacturers of the clock, J. B. Joyce & Co. Ltd, who agreed to dismantle and overhaul it in September 1953 for the sum of £50. This was agreed by the council.

The Chester Clock Today

When one considers the work that was required for what seems like a trifling sum, it is perhaps pertinent to highlight the wages paid to workmen at this time. Wages rose steeply throughout the 1950s from an average of just £5 8s a week, in 1951, to about £7 15s at the turn of the decade. In 1955, the average yearly wage was around £400.

Between 1951 and 1971, the workforce increased considerably, but mainly because more women came into full or part-time employment. Over this period, the character of employment in Chester also changed markedly. Whereas manufacturing and construction had employed 32 per cent of men and 19 per cent of women, in 1951, twenty years later they accounted for only 24 per cent and 6 per cent respectively. Altogether, by 1971, there were some 2,500 fewer manufacturing jobs in the city than in 1951, two thirds of them for men. On the other hand, the industrial sector in the wider region grew significantly and offered many opportunities for residents of Chester, but this was after the 1950s.

12,000 people worked at the Shotton steelworks. John Summers & Sons Ltd was a major United Kingdom iron and steel producer, which, during the 1950s was based at Shotton in Flintshire, just outside the city boundary. The company was nationalised in 1951, becoming part of the Iron and Steel Corporation of Great Britain, but was denationalised shortly afterwards, and then renationalised again in 1967.

The aforementioned Broughton factory of Hawker Siddeley employed around 4,000 and was established early in the Second World War as a shadow factory for Vickers-Armstrong Limited. The factory produced 5,540 Vickers Wellingtons and 235 Avro Lancasters. Post-war, the factory was used by Vickers to build planes and 28,000 aluminium prefab bungalows. Despite the name, Hawarden Airport is located in Broughton near Chester and not Hawarden in North Wales. It played a very important part as an RAF Station in the Second World War. The RAF's No. 48 Maintenance Unit was formed at Hawarden on 1 September 1939 and, until 1 July 1957, stored, maintained and scrapped many thousands of military aircraft, including the Handley Page Halifax, Wellingtons, Horsa gliders and De Havilland Mosquitoes. It was located on the north-west portion of the airfield. It is still in use as an airport today.

Broughton is still busy manufacturing aircraft wings, now as part of the Airbus UK Co., which employs over 5,000 people. Courtaulds had a factory in Flint, which manufactured manmade fibres and employed many Chester citizens.

RAF Sealand, on the Cheshire border, provided work for the people of Chester in the 1950s, at what had been a very busy RAF station during the war. After the war, in 1951, the station was taken over by the United States Air Force, and then handed back to the RAF in 1957.

Within the city boundaries, the Corporation provided a site for light industry at Sealand industrial estate in 1949, initially covering 30 acres and later extended. Eleven businesses were located there in 1960 and, by 1974, it had seventy firms employing up to 2,000 people. These services were mostly in distribution rather than manufacturing, as the importance of manufacturing to the city's economy had declined. In Chester in 1951, services including public utilities, transport, shops, financial services, public administration, hospitals, schools, hotels, and catering provided three in every five men's jobs, and four in every five women's.

Opposite Below: Outside Catering Staff from Bollands Restaurant, July 1958
Retailing was relatively stable – the number of shops remained about the same at over 850, although as supermarkets became established there were fewer food shops and more selling clothes, together with household goods and other non-food items. Chester had as much retail space as Ellesmere Port, a town of similar size, and more than Birkenhead, which had twice Chester's population. It placed Chester on a par with considerably larger county towns such as Oxford, Cambridge and Exeter. Sales in 1971 ran at around £640 per resident, far outstripping other towns in the region and similar towns elsewhere in England, though not by as much as in 1950.

Elsewhere in the service sector, numbers employed in hotels and catering fell in the 1950s, but nearly every other type of job became more numerous. There were 1,000 more jobs in banks, insurance companies and other financial services in 1971 than in 1951, and 4,500 more in education, medicine, the law, and other professions; both areas of employment had more than doubled in size. Chester's workforce was increasingly supplied from outside the city. Commuters into the county borough accounted for 37 per cent of the total employed by 1961. In the 1950s, employment was so buoyant that vacancies had to be filled from outside the area. By 1962, the Chester employment exchange area, which included parts of Tarvin and Chester rural districts and Hawarden rural district in Flintshire, had an unemployment rate of only 1.1 per cent, compared with 2.1 per cent nationally and 2.8 per cent in the North West region.

8

Chester's Historical Sites

Chester is famous for its historical sites and general antiquity, dating back to the Romans. First, we have to see how this history. Chester was founded as a 'castrum', or Roman fort, with the name *Deva Victrix*, in the year AD 79, by the Roman Legio II Adiutrix during the reign of the Emperor Vespasian. Chester's four main roads, Eastgate, Northgate, Watergate and Bridge Gate, follow routes laid out at this time. One of the three main Roman army camps, Deva later became a major settlement in the Roman province of Britannia.

Above: Site of Amphitheatre, 2010

Now we have a photograph of the excavated half of the amphitheatre, showing that, slowly but surely Chester's antiquities are now being preserved.

Opposite: Site of the Roman Amphitheatre, 1950s

Little St John Street curves around the north of the amphitheatre site, and contains the church of St John, once the Chester Cathedral. It was once known as Church Lane and Souter's Lane. The site of the amphitheatre seems to have long remained an open area where the citizens came to congregate, play and worship, becoming slowly filled in by natural erosion. It was sometime used as a refuse dump. A bear pit also provided a source of local 'amusement'. The arena was still visible as a shallow depression in the ground as late as 1710. Dee House was built in around 1730 as a town house for John Comberbach, a former Mayor of Chester. Extensions were made in the 1740s to the south and south-west, giving the house an L-shaped plan. It continued in use as a private residence until around 1850, when it was sold to the Church of England. In 1854, it passed to the Faithful Companions of Jesus, a religious institute of the Roman Catholic Church, who used it as a convent school. They added a wing to the east, which incorporated a chapel in its ground floor. In 1925, the building was taken over by the Ursulines, another religious institute. Dee House is still there and is sitting on part of the Roman amphitheatre. Within half a century, the northern half of this ancient gem had disappeared under houses, and the remains of the monument underneath quickly became lost.

So completely did it disappear,that W. Thompson Watkin, in his influential *Roman Cheshire of 1889*, wrote, 'There remains the interesting question, where was the amphitheatre? A station or castrum of the dimensions of *Deva* would certainly have one ... It would certainly, at Deva as elsewhere, be outside of the Roman walls, and I suspect either at Boughton or at the "Bowling Green."' This is the site of today's Roman Garden, just across Souter's Lane from the actual site. Local historians pondered the location of the amphitheatre, knowing that it was in Chester somewhere, but having no idea where it was. This was until a gardener from the Ursuline convent came across some stones during his gardening chores. He had found the Chester Roman Amphitheatre, which had been hidden completely for so long. One of the historians who visited the site was a classics teacher at the Chester King's School, W J 'Walrus' Williams (1875–1971), a keen amateur archaeologist. During the 1930s, battles raged with the council, who were of a mind to put a road across it. Ad hoc excavations continued until the 1950s and early 1960s, when excavations started on the small area that was not covered by buildings.

Amphitheatre So Far

After the fall of the Roman Empire, the Romano-British established a number of petty kingdoms in its place. Chester is thought to have been part of Powys at this time. King Arthur is said to have fought his ninth battle at the city of the legions, and St Augustine later came to the city to try and unite the church and hold his synod with the Welsh Bishops. In 616, Æthelfrith of Northumbria defeated a Welsh Army and probably established the Anglo-Saxon position in the area from then on.

In 689, the Minster church of West Mercia was founded on what is considered to be an early Christian site known as The Minster of St John the Baptist, Chester. This is still there, and is now St John's church. This church later became Chester's first cathedral, which we will look at later. A new church dedicated to St Peter alone was founded in AD 907, and some of its fabric dates from that time. The present church dates from the fourteenth, fifteenth and sixteenth centuries, with modifications added in the following three centuries. The tower originally had a spire, which was removed and rebuilt in the sixteenth century, taken down in the seventeenth century, then rebuilt and finally removed *c.* 1780, having suffered the effects of lightning over the years. During the Victorian years, the church was restored, and this restoration included the pyramid spire that we see today.

Church of St Peter, 1957

9

The Chester Cross

The Saxons extended and strengthened the walls of Chester to protect the city against the Danes, who occupied it for a short time until Alfred seized all the cattle and laid waste the surrounding land to drive them out. In fact, it was Alfred's daughter, known as the Lady of the Mercians, who built the new Saxon burh. The Anglo-Saxons called Chester Ceaster or Legeceaster. In 973, the Anglo Saxon Chronicle records that two years after his Coronation at Bath, King Edgar of England came to Chester, where he held his court in a place now known as Edgar's field, near the old Dee Bridge in Handbridge. Taking the helm of a barge, he was rowed the short distance up the River Dee from Edgar's field to the great Minster church of St John the Baptist. The rowers, according to the monk, Henry Bradshaw, were eight kings. Chester was one of the last towns in England to fall during the Norman Conquest, and William the Conqueror ordered the building of Chester Castle to protect the city from the Welsh.

Chester is one of the best-preserved walled cities in Britain. Apart from a 100-metre section, the walls are almost complete. The Industrial Revolution brought railways, canals, and new roads to the city, which saw substantial expansion and development. Chester played a significant part in this peaceful revolution, which began in the North West of England in the latter part of the eighteenth century. The city village of Newtown, located north-east of the city, was at the very heart of this industry. The large Chester cattle market, industrial sites along the canal, and the two Chester railway stations (Chester Northgate and Chester General), meant that this area was responsible for providing the vast majority of workers and, in turn, the vast amount of Chester's wealth production throughout the Industrial Revolution.

The Cross & Eastgate Street

The Chester Rows are unique in Britain. They consist of buildings with shops or dwellings on the lowest two storeys. The shops or dwellings on the ground floor are often lower than the street and are entered into by steps, which sometimes lead to a vault-like basement. Those on the first floor are entered behind a continuous walkway, often with a sloping shelf between the walkway and the railings overlooking the street. Much of the architecture of central Chester looks medieval. Most of the black-and-white buildings are a result of what Nikolas Pevsner termed the 'Black-and-White Revival'.

At the intersection of the former Roman roads in the city centre is Chester Cross or the Chester High Cross. It is a Grade II listed building dating from the fourteenth century. It was replaced with a new one in 1476 and gilded in 1603. Like similar crosses elsewhere in the area, it was damaged by the Parliamentarians in the Civil War, and the component parts spread around the county. After a search, the fragments were recovered in the nineteenth century and used in its restoration in 1949/50, after which it was re-erected at Chester's Newgate. Its final move was in 1975 when it was placed in or near its original position.

10

Chester Town Hall and Cathedral

The most prominent building in the city centre, apart from the cathedral, is the town hall, which was opened in 1869. It was built in Gothic Revival style with a tower and a short spire.

Above: Chester City Police Sub Division, 1953

This view of the Chester City Police Division was taken in early 1953 to mark the retirement of the Assistant Chief Constable Alexander Henderson, who is seated sixth from left. To his right is Superintendent Barney O'Sullivan, the divisional commander.

Prior to 1949, all towns with a suitably large population had their own police forces with Chief Constables but, in accordance with the Police Act of 1946, they were to be amalgamated into the Cheshire Constabulary. Forces such as Congleton and Macclesfield made the transition relatively painlessly, their chief constables becoming superintendents in the combined force. Chester, however, was slightly different, as it was a county borough with less than 100,000 population. In accordance with the rules, the Home Secretary ordered a public enquiry and then forcibly amalgamated the force into the Cheshire Constabulary on 1 April 1949 to become the Chester City Division. Note that the officers are wearing caps, which was the headgear in Cheshire from 1935 until 1964 when helmets were introduced. The old police station's cells in the town hall still exist, and old quarter sessions were held in this court until the abolition of quarter sessions by the Courts Act 1971. From then until 1993, it was used as a magistrates' court, with the adjoining room as a retiring room for the magistrates. One of the few remaining original Victorian courts in the country, it has been used in films, such as *Sherlock Holmes* and *Far from the Madding Crowd*.

Opposite: Chester Town Hall, 1914

In 1698, a market hall was built to accommodate the city's administrators, but this building burnt down in 1862. A competition was held to build a new town hall, and this was won by a gentleman named William Henry Lynn of Belfast. The building cost £40,000 and was officially opened on 15 October 1869 by the Prince of Wales, the future King Edward VII, who was accompanied by the Prime Minister, William Ewart Gladstone. On 27 March 1897, the council chamber on the second floor was gutted by fire and restored by Thomas Lockwood the following year. The building sits in Northgate Street and once had the prestigious Market Hall adjoining it. Until 1967, Chester's main police station was situated on the town hall's ground floor. In the 1950s, Chester had its own police force, the Chester City Police, under its own Chief Constable.

Former Magistrates' Court in the Town Hall, 1952

Here we have two photographs of the cathedral, one showing it in days gone by and the more modern one showing it with a flower bed laid out in the form of a medal as a tribute to those who fell fighting for the country.

Chester Cathedral, 1902

We look now at one of the major cathedrals in Britain, which, during the 1950s, was called upon by the folk of the city to celebrate peace and the new dawn. Its doors would see worshippers, tourists, royalty and the great and good, but where did it all start?

Chester Cathedral, 2014

Chester Cathedral is the mother church of the Diocese of Chester, and is located in the centre of the city. The cathedral was formerly the abbey church of a Benedictine monastery, which was dedicated to St Werburgh. Now, Chester's Cathedral is dedicated to Christ and the Blessed Virgin Mary.

Since 1541, it has been the seat of the Bishop of Chester. The cathedral is a Grade I listed building, and part of a heritage site that also includes the former monastery buildings to the north, which are also Grade I listed. Much of the interior is Norman in style and is considered to be the best example of eleventh- and twelfth-century church architecture in Cheshire. The cathedral has been modified many times from 1093 through to the present day. All the major styles of English medieval architecture are represented in the building today. One thing of note is the bishop's consistory court that is situated beneath the south-west tower, which is the last surviving example in England. The last case heard by the bishop therein was in the 1930s and dealt with the attempted suicide by a priest. Also in the cathedral is a memorial to John Travers Cornwell who, as a sixteen-year-old boy, was a seaman aboard HMS *Chester* and part of a gun crew during the battle of Jutland in 1916. All of the crew were killed, and he remained at his post until he also died. He was awarded a posthumous Victoria Cross, the third youngest serviceman to be honoured as such. A quick mention here of the man in charge of his squadron – Vice Admiral David Richard Beatty, from Stapeley near Nantwich.

The cathedral and former monastic buildings were again extensively restored during the nineteenth century, and a free-standing bell tower added in the twentieth century. The buildings are a major tourist attraction in Chester. In addition to holding services for Christian worship, the cathedral is now used as a venue for concerts and exhibitions. With the city of Chester an important Roman stronghold, there may have been a Christian place of worship on the site of the present cathedral in the late Roman era. As for St Werburgh, her body was brought to Chester in the ninth century and interred in the monastery. In 1538, at the time of the Dissolution of the Monasteries, the shrine was desecrated. Her name is still remembered in the street name of St Werburgh Street, which passes alongside the cathedral, and near to the city walls. In 1541, St Werburgh's abbey became a cathedral, and the dedication was changed to Christ and the Blessed Virgin. The Shrine of St Werburgh was reinstated in the nineteenth century.

11

The Golden Age of Fun and Frivolity

For many people, the 1950s was a golden age, and as the '50s dawned, it brought with it a new improvement in the life of Chester's residents. The demand for entertainment loomed large. During the war years, entertainment relieved the pressure and stress of the period and this continued after the last street party remains had been cleared away. Even before the jollities of the Coronation, people had begun to enjoy themselves with seaside holidays, such as the one taken by the residents of Heath Lane, who enjoyed a coach trip to Blackpool in the photograph below.

Opposite: Heath Lane Blackpool Trip, Early 1950s

Then came the Festival of Britain, which was a national exhibition held throughout the country in the summer of 1951. It was organised by the government to give Britons a feeling of recovery in the aftermath of the Second World War and to promote the British contribution to science, technology, industrial design, architecture and the arts. The Festival's centrepiece was in London on the South Bank of the River Thames, but there were events around the country, including Chester, where the Mystery Plays were revived as part of the Festival of Britain celebrations. A full-scale production has been produced every five years since.

To this day, the Chester Mystery Plays form a spectacular festival presented mainly by members of the local community under professional direction. This rare Chester production has become a much anticipated highlight in the British Arts calendar, attracting people from all over the world. One of the largest community events in the UK, hundreds of enthusiasts of all ages from throughout the area make up the cast, crew and the support teams working in administration/marketing and front of house.

Mystery Plays were created all across Europe from the thirteenth century as a means of celebrating the stories of the Old and New Testaments for the Feast of Corpus Christi. Other famous Mystery Play 'Cycles' in England were written in Coventry, York and Wakefield. The scripts, as in the case of the Chester Cycle, were often written by medieval monks. Originally performed inside the churches from the fourteenth century, they were produced by crafts guilds and performed in the open streets and market places on pageant wagons. Performed by local people, both scripts and performances changed each year to remain current and have popular appeal. The production of the plays, so important to the local community, was suppressed following the Reformation and the last recorded performance prior to the 1951 revival was in 1575.

VE Day in 1945 saw most streets in Britain throwing street parties, with mums and dads setting tables in the centre of the street and filling them with goodies. Naturally, there was also liquid refreshment for the adults, but in most cases the children took priority and the end of war was celebrated in style. Soon, there was another excuse for more street parties in the city, thanks to Princess Elizabeth being crowned Queen in 1953. Chester was not slow in coming forward.

Coronation Street Party, Nelson Street, June 1953

Here we see one of the many street parties that were held throughout the county for the Coronation. Music, merriment and fun could be found in Chester during the 1950s and various venues catered to this demand. There were plenty of dance halls and cinemas; one of the most popular dance hall venues of the time, described as 'a magic place', was Clemence's restaurant in Northgate Street.

Opposite: Len and Joan's Wedding Day

Clemence's Restaurant was located in Market Square, and good friend and excellent local historian, Len Morgan, and his wife, Joan, had their wedding reception here in 1955. They have kindly allowed me to use a photograph from the day, which was originally black and white, but Joan's expertise was used to coloured it by hand.

Below: Clemence's Restaurant

When you look at this photograph of Clemence's restaurant, you cannot but wonder how it came to be demolished to make way for a row of shops. The Wall (pun on Chester) City Jazzmen made their debut here on 18 January 1954. The format was to play Dixieland mainstream jazz and be as versatile as possible. The original band was really the Stan Roberts dance band, with Stan Roberts, piano; Tom Jones, trumpet; Ian Ashworth, trombone and tenor saxophone; John Nutthall, double bass and Alan Lewis, drums. Paul Blake was invited to make up the standard frontline on clarinet. Derek Masters and Don Davies promoted the band. Their intention was to provide an inexpensive post-weekend evening for young people. It was so successful that other bands were promoted for the evenings. These included the Freddie Render band and the Merseysippi Jazz Band.

THE ORIGINAL WALL CITY JAZZMEN C. 1957

Alan Lewis

Joe Nuttal

Stan Roberts

Pete Wright

Ian Ashwo...

...m Jones

Paul Blake

Wall City Jazzmen, 1950s

Late in 1954, Gordon Vickers asked the Jazzmen if they would be the resident band at his proposed Wall City Jazz Club at Quaintways, which was in the same street as the old venue. The band agreed and this club opened about six months later. It was at this venue that a sixteen-year-old Pete Wright joined the band as a featured 'Skiffle' singer and guitarist. In 1958, fifteen-year-old Trish Fields joined the band. Later, she turned professional and won the TV *New Faces* with a band called Whiskey Mac. Both the Wall City Jazzmen and Trish have their names in bricks on the Cavern Wall of Fame at Liverpool's Mathew Street. Guest artists over the years included Earl Hines, Vic Dickinson, Edmund Hall, Bud Freeman and many more. It also became quite normal for the band to play at jazz venues in London (clubs like George Webb's Hot Club, the Fishmonger's Arms and Cooks Ferry), as well as concerts at the Shakespeare and Empire theatres in Liverpool. There were also gigs at provincial clubs such as St George's Hall, Blackburn, and the Dudley Hippodrome, among many others. On 16 January 1957, Alan Sytner featured the band, along with the Merseysippi Jazz Band and the Ralph Watmough Band, at the opening of the Cavern in Liverpool, soon to succumb to Skiffle and the Quarrymen, later known as The Beatles.

The Wall City Jazz Club also had a great deatl of success at Quaintways. Over the twenty years that the band played there, the scene gradually changed from the great British jazz bands and American guests, such as Earl Hines, to a more 'rock' orientated venue. Guests at this time included such bands as Long John Baldry's Steam Packet with Judy Driscoll (vocals), Elton John (keyboards) and a young Rod Stewart fronting. One foggy night, Fleetwood Mac was booked, but the evening had very few customers. Quaintways eventually closed, only to open again as a nightclub. At the time of writing, the Wall City Jazz band still perform every Monday at the Mill Hotel & Spa, Milton Street, Chester.

Dennis Williams Quintet, 1950s

Another band popular at Clemence's Restaurant in the 1950s was the Dennis Williams Quintet. This band performed every Thursday and Saturday in the small dance hall at the rear of the restaurant. Not quite as famous asthe Wall City Jazz Men, perhaps, but a very popular band at the time.

The King's Arms Tavern stood at No. 2 Union Street, opposite the end of Love Street. This was another venue popular for dancing and merriment, and also had connections with The Beatles. After closing it became the Grosvenor skating rink (it seems to have been extensively enlarged rearwards at this time) and then the Broadway Dancing Academy Ballroom, nicknamed 'The Ack'. It was a favourite haunt of American servicemen stationed around Chester during the Second World War and became The Riverpark ballroom.

Opposite above: Riverpark Ballroom Union Street, 1950s

The Riverpark Ballroom was opposite the baths in Union Street and was built in 1931 on the site of an earlier pub called The King's Arms. It was then called the Grosvenor Roller Skating Rink. In 1935, it was renamed The Broadway Palace Dancing Academy but was better known as 'The Ack'. In 1952, it was renovated and renamed the Riverpark Ballroom. In the 1950s, Gene Mayo, Al Powell and Paul Vaughan were regular bands playing there. The Ray Ellington Quartet, with singer Marion Ryan, also played there. Marion's sons, Paul and Barry Ryan, went on to fame and fortune in their own right in the 1960s. The Beatles played one of their Chester dates here on 16 August 1962. Their original but freshly sacked drummer, Pete Best was supposed to play his final gig that night, but, unsurprisingly, he didn't bother turning up, and had to be hastily replaced with Johnny Hutchinson. The first Beatles concert with Ringo behind the drum kit, at Hulme Hall in Birkenhead, took place two nights later. The Riverpark Ballroom closed the following year and today the site is occupied by NatWest's nondescript offices.

The record industry, radio and television industries completely changed in the 1950s. Music drifted slowly but inexorably towards rock 'n' roll and pop, the days of the crooners and the big bands in mainstream popularity drawing slowly to an end. Although quite a wealthy city, few people in Chester had television sets until the decade was well under way, so it was down to radio to entertain both at home and in the workplace. Shows like *Workers Playtime* had the factories and front rooms singing along to the music of the day. A few artistes of that time would turn up at a factory canteen and entertain the workers live. Singers in the fifties were not accompanied by big bands and technology, but rather a pianist in between male comedians such as Ted Ray, Tommy Trinder, Arthur Askey, Charlie Chester and many others.

Female entertainers, such as Ruby Murray, Patti Page and Doris Day, made records and performed on the radio and the new medium of television. People were treated to programmes like *Two Way Family Favourites* and *The Billy Cotton Bandshow*, followed by a comedy series at lunchtime like as *The Navy Lark* with Lesley Phillips, then *Hancock's Half Hour*, *Life with the Lyon's* and *Beyond our Ken*, later to become *Around the Horne* with Kenneth Horne. There wasn't much experimentation on the radio and censorship was strict. The country was just regaining its feet after a catastrophic war, and the Cold War was just kicking off. Everyone expected the world to end at any second, so the strictly controlled BBC and its stuffy management ensured that the public enjoyed what they felt they should enjoy. This went on until rock 'n' roll arrived and gave the stuffed shirts a good kicking. Morning radio was targeted at wives and mothers because working mothers were almost unheard of, with programmes such as *Housewives Choice*, *Music While you Work* and *Mrs Dales Diary*. On TV in the evenings, there would be quiz shows such as *Take Your Pick* with Michael Miles, panel shows like *The Brains Trust* and then the *Grove Family* – one of the first of a long line of family soap operas. Jazz continued to buck the trend all the time, with Chester dance halls leaning heavily upon it. We have already featured the most successful Jazz band from Chester, The Wall City Jazz Band, but down at Clemence's Restaurant there was always the Roy Williams Band to enjoy.

Who can forget *In Town Tonight*? Made during the height of 1950s technology, Piccadilly Circus was brought to a halt as the intro played. As the 1950s progressed, so did the acquisition of television sets with their little screens and big cases. 1952 saw the first of the *I Love Lucy* series with Lucille Ball, *What's My Line?* in 1950, *Dixon of Dock Green* in 1955 and *The Ed Sullivan Show*, which ran from 1949 to 1971 – all featuring the stars of the day.

Opposite below: Roy Williams Band, 1957

Roy Williams played with a few bands and notable musicians. For instance, the man on the trumpet in this 1957 photograph is Syd Lawrence. Syd actually comes from Wilmslow and was brought up in Shotton on the Chester border. He played at The Vaughan Hall in Shotton, which at that time was a dance hall, and later formed a quintet to play at Clemence's. This photograph is more recent than that and probably features him as a guest.

The Old Lamb Stores and the Falcon, 1950s

Venues for the youth of the 1950s tended to be coffee bars or milk bars and, in Chester, the most notable of these was above what was known locally as The Dive. This nickname had a very innocent source; to enter, anyone of normal height would have to duck or dive to prevent a bang on the head. The building seen in the photograph was situated at the top of Lower Bridge Street next to the ancient Falcon Hotel, which is still there. Prior to its construction, the site was occupied by Old Lamb Row. It was a timber building whose upper storey protruded so far over the street, and whose creaking beams sagged so amazingly that it quickly achieved a reputation as being Chester's most picturesque building and was portrayed by many visiting artists. It was originally constructed as the home of historian and heraldic artist Randle Holme III in 1655, but was later converted into shops, a market and finally into an inn (The Lamb Inn), which gave its name to the long-vanished Lamb Row. So dilapidated was the structure, however, that the whole building inevitably collapsed into the street in 1821. The *Chester Chronicle* reported at the time, 'this ancient pile, like all the works of man, underwent a severe shock from the hands of time ... the projecting portion of the south end suddenly gave way and tumbled into the street with a loud crash. An immense volume of dust rose from the ruins, and it was some time before bystanders could ascertain what damage was done and whether any injury had been sustained'.

The Old Lamb Stores and the Falcon from Lower Bridge Street, c. 1959

Another photograph, now from 1959, shows the building when looking up Lower Bridge Street. The building that rose on the site of Old Lamb Row was, for a long time, the home of Brooksbank's wine dealers, the 'Old Lamb Stores', with a pub, The Dive, beneath. This building, in its turn, was demolished in 1964 to make way for the Inner Ring Road. Little Cuppin Street, the narrow lane that ran between the Lamb and the even more ancient (but thriving) Falcon Inn, also vanished at this time of great change. Few surveying the scene today would suspect that buildings had stood here for hundreds of years.

A mention of the Falcon itself would not go amiss here. The building started life as a house around 1200 and was later extended to the south along Lower Bridge Street, with a great hall running parallel to the street. During the thirteenth century, it was rebuilt to incorporate its portion of the row. It was rebuilt again during the late sixteenth and early seventeenth centuries and in 1602 was bought by Sir Richard Grosvenor, who extensively altered it some forty years later to make it his town house. During the English Civil War, he moved his family here from his country home at Eaton Hall. In 1643, Sir Richard petitioned the city assembly for permission to enlarge his house by enclosing the portion of the row that passed through his property. This was successful and it set a precedent for other residents of Lower Bridge Street to enclose their portion of the rows, or to build new structures that did not incorporate the rows. As a result, that street no longer has rows, unlike the rest of the city centre. In the late eighteenth century, the building ceased to be the town house of the Grosvenor family, although it continued in their ownership. Between 1778 and 1878, it was licensed as the Falcon Inn.

Next Store, Site of Chester's First Cinema

Chester's First Cinema, Now a Next Store

In the 1950s, cinema became very popular, and Chester boasted several such establishments. The first of these was this building. In 1904, it was the headquarters of Dickson's Seed Merchants, whose seed nursery was in Dickson Drive, Newton. The entrance on the right under the Corn Exchange sign was also the entrance to Chester's first silent movie cinema, The Picturedrome, which opened on 8 November 1909 and closed on 29 March 1924. It was a Woolworths for many years and is now a branch of Next.

One cinema open in the 1950s was The Majestic, or, as known by the children of the 1950s, The Bug Hutch. It was built by Pat Collins of Pat Collins Fairground fame, who was born in Steven Street, Boughton. 1950s children would enjoy such delights as Hopalong Cassidy, Roy Rogers and science fiction in the form of Flash Gordon.

Staff of the Majestic Cinema, Early 1950s

Here is a photograph of the staff at The Majestic – how many naughty children did these good folk have to tell off? The Majestic closed in 1956 and opened as The Majestic Ballroom with the Peter Dee band in residence; after that it became the Top Rank bingo hall.

Saltney had its own cinema called The Park, located in Coronation Street. It boasted what were nicknamed 'love seats': two seats together with no armrest in between, making a bit of cuddling easy. This cinema opened in 1923 and closed on 2 May 1959, the last film being *Camp on Blood Island*.

Regal Cinema

Chester's last big cinema, prior to the multiplex type, was in Foregate Street and was called the Regal. It was opened by the Mayor of Chester, who at the time was Robert Mathewson. The date was Saturday 30 October 1937. The opening film at the 1,973-seat cinema was *Slave Ship*, starring Warner Baxter, which can be seen advertised on the photograph from the time. On 10 August 1953, the Regal presented the 3D film, *House of Wax*, which played for two weeks. This had audiences ducking as images appeared to leap out at them. Special cardboard glasses with coloured cellophane lenses had to be worn. Another 3D film was *13 Ghosts*. The novelty did not last long and the cinema has only just had modern technology reintroduced. In 1959, the name Regal was dropped and from then on it was just called ABC.

Gaumont Palace Cinema from Cow Lane Bridge, 1952

In this 1952 photograph we see the Gaumont Palace cinema in Brook Street. The photograph was taken from Cow Lane Bridge. The cinema was built specifically for sound in 1931 and seated 2,000 people. It was the only Chester cinema to house a restaurant, and this was a luxurious Tudor-style affair called The Oak Restaurant. It was open all day for patrons and non-patrons to dine. The cinema was popular through the 1950s and did not finally close its doors until 9 December 1961, with the last film being *The Marriage Go Round*. It went on to be a bowling alley and a Top Rank bingo hall, taking over from the old Majestic.

Royalty Theatre City Road, 1950

The Chester Royalty Theatre in City Road was built in 1882 on the site of an earlier, wooden building that was used as a makeshift theatre. It was originally called the Oxford Music Hall, but the reason for this is lost in the mists of time, as it soon changed its name to the Prince of Wales. Eventually, the wooden structure was replaced with a brick-built, 2,000-seat building called the New Royalty Theatre, which was built by Bleakley & Son of Birkenhead. City Road, which linked the new railway station, Chester General, with Foregate Street, had itself only been laid out just over twenty years earlier. The new theatre's street address was Nos 20–24 City Road.

In December 1915, a fatal accident occurred on stage when a Japanese acrobatic troupe, the Mikado Family, were performing their act. Twenty-three-year-old Ishiao Ishimura failed to complete a somersault and landed on the stage on the back of his neck. He was transferred to the Chester Infirmary, where he died the following day. He was laid to rest in the large cemetery near to the Grosvenor bridge, where his grave can still be seen with its inscription in both Japanese and English. In 1957, Dennis Critchley became director and general manager. He was responsible for production and direction of the theatre's own plays, shows and pantomimes. He also controlled the booking of all touring productions that appeared. Russ Abbott, whose brother had a pub in Chester, was subject of a *This is your Life* programme in 1997, during which he thanked Dennis Critchley personally for teaching him the rudiments of comedy presentation and timing. During the 1950s, many variety stars such as Ken Dodd, Jimmy Young, Harry Worth and Frankie Vaughan performed at the Royalty.

In 1957, builder Frank White undertook extensive structural alterations to the theatre; cantilever-type balconies replaced the older designs that can be seen in the photograph, their ornate plasterwork and pillars were removed to improve visibility. Boxes at each side of the stage were also removed at this time. Meet Mr Callaghan was the first production to be performed in the refurbished hall. This was opened on 8 July 1957 by the theatre historian W. McQueen Pope. Because of declining audience numbers, allegedly due to the rising popularity of cinema and then of television, the old theatre was forced to close in 1966 after a continuous run of eighty-four years. It was later demolished and the site now houses a new Premier Inn.

Bolland's Oyster Bar, Early 1950s

Bolland's Oyster Bar was a licensed restaurant at No. 42 Eastgate Street, next to Brown's of Chester and opposite the Boot Inn. One regular customer was Roland Cutler, who was twenty-three in 1956, and who reminisced about Bolland's in the local press:

We used to go to Bolland's for a drink, then across to The Boot and then come back to have a meal in the Horseshoe Bar, where you could get fine ham and eggs for five shillings. It was a monkey run for the men – you found yourself a girl and then went to dance with her in Clemence's. Anyone who went to the races would go to Bolland's for oysters beforehand. It was a beautiful bar.

King's Arm's Kitchen

Another interesting pub during the 1950s was the King's Arms Kitchen. As you look towards the Eastgate Street Clock from within the walls on the left-hand side, immediately next to the gate is a narrow passageway, at present locked with an iron door. At the end of this, there formerly existed a public house called the King's Arms Kitchen, also known as Mother Halls. In the eighteenth and ninteenth centuries, it housed a drinking and gambling club by the splendid name of The Honorable Incorporation of the King's Arm's Kitchen. This came about as the result of an order by King Charles II, which saw the ancient custom of electing the mayor and his officers come to an end. Sir Thomas Grosvenor was appointed as mayor, thus spawning an oligarchy between Eaton Hall (the Grosvenor residence) and Chester Corporation, which would last until the Election Reform Act of 1832.

The city's people were, unsurprisingly, increasingly unhappy with this imposition of an unelected mayor and Corporation, and one evening around the year 1770, a group of tradesmen met in a room in this pub and decided to form a city assembly of their own. This was organised as a complete shadow assembly, a satirical imitation of the Corporation, with its own elected mayor, recorder, town clerk, sheriffs, aldermen and common councilmen. They even had a replica of the mayor's sword and mace made for them. In the course of time, the serious, satirical point of the King's Arms Kitchen was largely lost and it degenerated into a drinking and gambling club. The regulars, however, did not forget the old rules and regulations, which declared that if a stranger sat in the mayor's chair, it was his duty to buy drinks for all present. During the Second World War, many an American GI was invited to sit in the imposing chair, only to have to buy drinks all round.

When the King's Arms Kitchen closed in 1978, the chairs, plaques and a display of this unique pub room were removed to the Grosvenor museum, where it can still be seen.

12

Chester Railways

Chester General Station, 2014

Chester once had two stations in the city, with others in the outlying villages. The main station was, and still is, Chester General station, which was a joint station and included the Holyhead Railway, the Chester Crewe railway and the Birkenhead Railway. Later, these became part of the massive London & North West Railway (LNWR) and the Great Western Railway (GWR). This joint station dates from 1848. Architecturally, the station has an Italianate frontage and was designed by Francis Thompson. The station also has carved wooden owls at some strategic locations high in the roof beams to help deter pigeons.

Chester Northgate Station, 1950s

During the 1950s, and prior to the later Beeching cuts, Chester General was the main Chester station and the gateway to North Wales, the Irish boats from Holyhead and trains from London and throughout the country. Chester Northgate station was built in 1875 and was owned by the Cheshire Lines Committee (CLC). This station was the Western Terminus of the CLC line from Manchester to Chester via Northwich. The station was more convenient for local traffic than Chester General and was soon connected to Birkenhead, the Wirral and North Wales. It was given a new roof by British Railways in 1950, and in January 1960, it was closed to steam engines (after that date only Diesel Multiple Units used it). In this photograph, the new roof is visible. The station was completely demolished on 6 October 1969, all of the lines were lifted and now the Northgate Arena, Chester's sports complex, occupies the site.

CHESTER

Above: Saughall Station, Closed in 1954

Now we have a long-lost station in Mickle Trafford, which opened to traffic in December 1889 and closed on 12 February 1951. In this photograph, we see an excursion to New Brighton. These small country stations still enjoyed a wealth of manpower. Here, the stationmaster, in his fine uniform, is with two other members of staff, probably porters. This station was situated on the Manchester to Chester line, although the line now enters Chester General and not Chester Northgate.

Opposite: Railway Poster from the 1950s

The outlying stations can be seen here. Firstly, Saughall station, which was opened on 16 March 1896 and closed on 1 February 1954. It was on the line from Chester Northgate to Hawarden, via Sealand, Connah's Quay and Shotton. It is a typically pretty station building, technically situated on the Welsh border and later serving the RAF base at Sealand. The station also served trains from the Wirral such as Egremont, Wallasey and New Brighton. The track bed is now a pleasant country walk.

Mickle Trafford Station

Mickle Trafford station was opened in 1889 by the Birkenhead Joint Railway on the Chester to Warrington line. On 2 April 1951 it closed completely. The Cheshire Lines Railway from Chester to Manchester ran close by it, but the lines were not joined until 1942 when Mickle Trafford was linked to the CLC line and became a junction. The area remains a busy junction today, catering for trains from Chester General to Manchester, via Northwich, and Chester General to Manchester, via Warrington. All signs of the actual station have now disappeared. In in this *c*. 1920s photograph, we see the staff posing for the photographer while waving off a local train. Note the communication cord running along the roof, albeit not appearing to be as continuous as it should be.

Emergency brakes were introduced in the United Kingdom by the Regulation of Railways Act 1868. Section 22 stated, 'All trains travelling a distance of more than 20 miles without stopping are to be provided with a means of communication between the passengers and the servants of the company in charge of the train'. At first, this means of communication was a cord running down the length of the train at roof level outside the carriages, connected to a bell on the locomotive as in this photograph. When the use of automatic brakes was made compulsory by the Regulation of Railways Act 1889, the equipment was modified so that it operated the brakes. This remained the case until 1948, when an express was stopped at Winsford by a soldier, who was once a signalman at Winsford signal box, and who pulled the communication cord to get off near his home. It became a contributory factor in a fatal collision. Now a pulled cord reverts to the original plan of simply alerting the train staff.

13

Chester Shops

Lower Bridge Street, 1956

Retail sales were far higher in 1950 than in any other town or city in an area stretching as far as Liverpool and Manchester. They were also higher than in comparable county and resort towns elsewhere. Chester has always been a Mecca for tourists, and after the war this trade resumed in the 1950s, with tourists travelling in to immerse themselves in all that this vibrant city had to offer. This ranged from walking the walls and retail therapy, to ancient pubs, museums and the enjoyment that could be had boating on the Dee.

Maypole Arthur Walls, Mid-1950s

In the 1950s, until the introduction of supermarkets and then out of town shopping, Chester was filled with small shops selling all sorts of goods. Here is a mid-1950s example of what the Rows looked like in those days. We can see a Ford Thames 300E delivery van owned by A. Wall & Sons parked in Watergate near to The Cross. The logo on the side of the van gives the address as The Cross. Next to it is the Maypole grocers' store, one of a chain of stores in the 1950s. In fact, my mother worked in one of them in Liverpool. This was part of a chain of grocers known as the Maypole Dairy Co. and the first shop in the chain was opened in 1887 in Wolverhampton. These shops are situated near to The Cross and show the Chester Rows quite clearly with upper and lower shops. Chester is the only city in the world with such a configuration. The Victoria pub is on the row above these shops. The main shopping street for the last few centuries was Eastgate Street, with the famous Eastgate Clock celebrating Queen Victoria's Jubilee above the gate.

Two Woolworths Stores, 1951

How many people alive in the 1950s can forget Woolworths? That familiar smell and the presents that one would buy from there at Christmas and birthdays. Well, in Chester it appears that you get two 'Woolies' for the price of one, so to speak. Although in the photograph there appear to be two Woolworths, in fact, although separated by two other premises, the two Woolworths did link up inside. In this photograph from 1951, a policeman is directing traffic in a scene filled with period charm. The car behind the Vauxhall Velox is a relatively new Morris Minor, which was termed the 'Low Light' due to the position of the headlights; these would soon be altered and placed higher up in the redesigned front wings. The Eastgate was once the main entrance into Chester and was built in 1769 to replace an earlier and narrower structure. As for Woolworths, this gem of our heritage and childhood memories closed its doors in the UK in 2009, but the memories live on. The Woolworth name survived in Germany, Austria, South Africa and Mexico and, until the start of 2009, in the United Kingdom.

The F. W. Woolworth Co. was simply referred to as Woolworths, or more colloquially, Woolies, and was a retail company that was once, arguably, the most successful American and international store in the world. Originally known as the 'Five & Dime store', it set trends and created the modern retail model followed by stores worldwide today. The first Woolworths, opened by Frank Winfield Woolworth, on 22 February 1878 as 'Woolworth's Great Five Cent Store' in New York. Though it initially appeared to be successful, the store soon failed. Ftank brought in his brother, Charles Sumner Woolworth, who went by the nickname 'Sum', into the business. The two Woolworth brothers pioneered and developed the merchandising, direct purchasing, sales and customer service practices that are commonly used today.

But what of this excellent photograph filled with antiquity, picturing shops in the city centre, some of which have now disappeared. In this image you will find Mac Fisheries, Kardomah, B. Walton & Sons Jewellers and Martins Bank. All of this is under the watchful eye of the Chester Eastgate, which has been there since it was built twenty years before the French Revolution in 1769, replacing an even older medieval gate. Chester really has so much to offer.

Browns of Chester, 2010

Browns of Eastgate Street was Chester's premier department store, which had a staff of over 600 and was situated on the opposite side of the road to Woolworths during the 1950s. The department store, known as 'the Harrods of the North', is still trading today. It was established in 1780 by Susannah Brown, and the store has traded from its current site since 1791. The building interior contains many ornate features, such as glass domed roofs and elaborate plasterwork surrounding small chandeliers in the main entrance area. On the second floor, parts of the glass roof have been concealed, as it has been covered by the construction of the third-floor extension containing the main café and Kalmora Spa. It can still be seen by carefully looking through the suspended ceiling now covering it. The Crypt Chambers, which is the stone building to the right of the painted one in the photograph, is the oldest part of the store. It was designed by pioneer architect T.M. Penson, whose portfolio included many spectacular buildings in the Cheshire Shropshire and North Wales areas, including Shrewsbury railway station, other buildings in Eastgate Street and the Queens and Grosvenor hotels in Chester. It is a Grade I listed building.

Crypt Chambers is built on the site of a house where the undercroft is still present. The building incorporates part of the Chester Rows. On the front of the tower, at Row level, is a blank scroll; on the east face is a recessed panel containing the initials W. B. (for William Brown); on the west face are the initials C. B. (for Charles Brown); and on the rear face is a scroll inscribed 'AD 1858, Crypt Chambers'. The Gothic façade frontage is built over a medieval undercroft dating from the twelfth century. The undercroft currently contains the Tea Press tea room. The architectural historian, Nikolas Pevsner, considered its undercroft to be 'one of the best medieval crypts of Chester'.

Old Market Hall, 1890s

Like most towns and cities, Chester has a market hall. As can be seen in the photograph from the 1890s, it was attached to the town hall and just as attractive a building in its own way. It was built in a Baroque Revival style in 1863, replacing three inns that had long occupied the site: the White Lion (Chester's premier coaching inn for over two centuries), the Saracen's Head and the Boot Tavern. Its presence doubtlessly influenced the design of the new town hall, which commenced two years later, in 1865, with which it harmonised perfectly. Both buildings were as one and greatly enhanced the look of the Market Hall.

The Forum Shopping Centre

Market Hall remained until the late 1950s/1960s, until the superb building was demolished and it was replaced with a scrappy lump of 1960s nastiness. Like most 1960s designs, it has since been half demolished so that they could try again. In the 1950s, Chester folk could (for a short while at least) enjoy the old Market Hall. Here are is one of the stalls that the building contained.

James Dandy & Son, Chester Market, 1950s

This photograph is of James Dandy, whose sons were James Dandy of Hill Farm, Guilden Sutton, and Sid Dandy of Park Farm, Guilden Sutton. The produce sold on the stall came from the farms. The stall had a spectacular display, typical of some of the other stalls in the market during the 1950s, a fashion that has unfortunately gone out of favour. The Dandy family were long-standing market traders.

Siddall and English Leather Bridge Street, 1950s

Another example of a Chester shop in the 1950s is J. D. Siddall. This company was formed in Chester in 1815, and in 1934 it was based at No. 4 Bridge Street, by The Cross. In this 1950s photograph, the company is still based at No. 4 Bridge Street. In a perfect example of longevity, it is still in the same premises. In the 1934 directory, the company is advertised as being the opticians to the Chester Royal Infirmary, along with being a scientific instrument and umbrella maker. Another ancient trade in Chester was leather, with tanneries in Foregate Street, and also in between St John's church and the river. Next door to J. D. Siddall, we can see the business of English Leather Co. Ltd. Again, checking the 1934 directory, we find this business at that location advertising themselves as footwear specialists.

14

Tourism

During the 1950s, Chester resumed attracting tourists from far and wide, with so much to offer in the way of ancient sites: a famous zoo, museums, the Roodee and its air of genteel antiquity. This is the secret of Chester's success and why it is one of the premier places for city breaks in the country. It is not one thing but a combination of all things that people find attractive, and there is simply something for everyone – the urban sophistication of the Rows, the racing at the Roodee and the ancient pubs, cathedral and river. But all of these visitors, both foreign and from nearer home, require somewhere to stay, and therein lies another employer for the locals. Chester has many hotels and guest houses, from the upmarket Grosvenor hotel in Eastgate Street to the bijou guest houses in Hoole, all welcoming the Chester visitor.

Above: Rowton Hall Hotel

The Grosvenor is particularly worthy of note, but other Chester hotels are of historical interest. One of these hotels is Rowton Hall Hotel, which is just 1 mile from Chester city centre. The hall was originally built in the fourteenth century and was rebuilt in 1779 in the Georgian style. It stands on the historic Rowton Moor – the site of a major battle of the English Civil War between the Royalists and Parliamentarians, where the Royalists were significantly defeated. Chester was King Charles' only remaining port and he observed the battle from Chester's walls. Royalist casualties were high, with 600 killed and 900 taken prisoner. This defeat prevented Charles from relieving the defenders in Chester, which fell to the Parliamentarians on 3 February 1646.

The hall was established as a hotel in 1955. It still retains many of the features of the original building, including extensive oak panelling, a self-supporting hand-carved staircase, an original inglenook fireplace and an elegant Robert Adam fireplace.

Opposite: The Grosvenor Hotel, 2010

Grosvenor is the Duke of Westminster's family name, which explains features in the city such as the Grosvenor Bridge and the Grosvenor Park. Much of Chester's architecture dates from the Victorian era, many of the buildings being modelled on Jacobean architecture. The building's half-timbered style was designed by Cheshire architect John Douglas, who was employed by the Duke as his principal architect. He had a trademark of twisted chimney stacks, many of which can be seen on the buildings in the city centre. Among other buildings Douglas designed, the Chester public baths. Another feature of all buildings, belonging to the estate of Westminster, is the 'Grey Diamonds' – a weaving pattern of grey bricks in the red brickwork laid out in a diamond formation.

Just by the Eastgate clock was the Grosvenor hotel, now known as The Chester Grosvenor. It is a Grade II listed building nd is owned by the Duke of Westminster. Before the present building was constructed, the site was occupied first by the Golden Talbot pub. In 1784, the pub was demolished to make way for The Royal Hotel, built by the politician and landowner the 1st Baron Crewe. It became the headquarters of the Independent Party, who were opposed to the Grosvenor family. In 1815, it was purchased by Robert Grosvenor, who was at that time Earl Grosvenor and later became the 1st Marquess of Westminster. It was then renamed the Grosvenor Hotel, and it became the city's 'premier place to stay'. While it was in possession of the 1st Marquess' son, Richard Grosvenor, in 1863, this building was demolished, and the building now present on the site, again originally called the Grosvenor Hotel, was built. The hotel passed into the estate of the Duke of Westminster when Richard's son, Hugh Grosvenor, was advanced to 1st Duke of Westminster in 1874. The Chester Grosvenor is the only five star hotel in Chester, and was as popular in the 1950s as it is today.

15

Newtown, Chester & The Industrial Revolution

St Anne Street, Newtown, 1959

Newtown, located north-east of the city and bounded by the Shropshire Union Canal, was at the very heart of the Industrial Revolution in Chester. The large Chester cattle market, and the two Chester railway stations, meant that Newtown, Chester, with its cattle market and canals, and Hoole, with its railways, were responsible for providing the vast majority of workers. This saw a vast amount of Chester's wealth sourced from the Industrial Revolution. Newtown had been increasing in size and importance to the Chester economy from around 1793, when the canal in Chester was finished, through to the late 1950s, when the last flour mill on the canal closed. Grffiths Bros' Mill, shown in the next photograph, was later converted into the Mill Hotel.

The area supported a thriving community of artisans and working-class families who lived mainly in 'two-up-two-down' terraced housing, with no bathroom and an outside toilet. Due to the location of the canal and, later, due to the great railway building of the 1830s and 1840s in Great Britain, Chester (Newtown) became the centre of northern English commerce.

Griffiths Mill Near Sellar Street, 2009

The canal was the 'motorway' of its day and narrowboats carried produce and supplies to and from North Wales (coal, slate, gypsum and lead ore). Finished lead (for roofing, water pipes and sewerage) produced in the huge leadworks factory in Edgerton Street, Newtown, was exported all over the country. Grain arrived from Cheshire farmland and was processed in the large granaries on the banks of the canal at Newtown and Boughton, and salt (for preserving food such as fish and meat) came in from Northwich. All of this was to cease in the 1950s.

Canal & Methodist Hall, 1959

Here we have a photograph of the Chester Canal in the 1950s. It was taken by the bridge crossing by the steam mill. The Gothic Methodist Central Hall can be seen on the left. This was built in 1873 as a Methodist chapel at a cost of £8,000, and was demolished in the 1970s. The Chester Canal linked Nantwich town with the River Dee. It was intended to link Chester to Middlewich (with a branch to Nantwich), but the Trent & Mersey Canal Co. were uncooperative regarding a junction at Middlewich, and so the route to Nantwich was opened in 1779. There were also difficulties negotiating with the River Dee Co. and, with no possibility of through traffic, the canal was uneconomic. Part of it was closed in 1787 when Beeston staircase locks collapsed, and there was no money to fund repairs. When the Ellesmere Canal was proposed in 1790, the company saw it as a ray of hope, and somehow managed to keep the struggling canal open. The Ellesmere Canal provided a link to the River Mersey at Ellesmere Port from 1797, and the fortunes of the Chester Canal began to improve. The canals were nationalised in 1948, and long-distance commercial traffic struggled on through the 1950s. By 1958, it had all but ended, relinquishing its place in history to pleasure craft.

Above: The Canal Viewed from Cow Lane Bridge, 1957

Another look at the canal and the Griffiths Bros Mill in 1957. This view is from Cow Lane Bridge at the strangely named Gorse Stacks area of Chester. This name refers to the stacks of gorse for kindling that were stored there to supply the city. The name Cow Lane comes from the cattle market that was once nearby.

Opposite below: 'Dandys', 1950s

This photograph of fishermen opposite what was known locally as Dandy's Shed was taken in 1955. The red, corrugated iron building was operated by Mr William Herbert Horne in 1934, who was a Canal Carrier of Cambrian Road. The name seems to have come into local use in the late 1950s when James Arthur Dandy took over the building and yard for his long established haulage business. The firm moved premises in the late 1990s and the shed was demolished. The company went on to be known as 'Dandy's Topsoil', a well known and respected local business, dealing in all forms of topsoil, gravel and coal, and now based at Sealand Road, Chester.

Abbey Square & the Old King's School Buildings, 1951

The prestigious King's School was situated in buildings adjoining the north-west corner of the cathedral. These dedicated school buildings were opened by William Ewart Gladstone in 1876. During the 1940s, pupil numbers rose and the school took over part of the former Bluecoat School buildings on Upper Northgate Street. By the early 1950s, a 999-syear lease had been secured with the Eaton Estate for the current 32-acre site on Wrexham Road on the outskirts of the city. Design of the buildings started in 1956, and in 1960, the whole school moved to the new site.

Lower Watergate, St Trinity Church (Later Guildhall), 1956

Another home of learning in the 1950s was the Chester College of Further Education, and during the early 1950s, a single-site campus was planned for a college to be spread out on five sites around the city. The school of art used the Grosvenor Museum. The majority of technical classes such as carpentry, joinery, plumbing and motor vehicle technology were taught in buildings situated on Queen's Park Road, Handbridge. The most interesting of these premises was the bakery school, which, in the 1950s, was installed on the ground floor of No. 30 Watergate Street where Mr Ricketts, the senior bakery instructor, taught classes to students studying towards City & Guilds qualifications in bread making and flour confectionery. In the photograph, we see the entrance to Watergate Street in 1956, with a view of the old Trinity church that, like many Chester churches, would go on to fulfil another role (in this case it became the Chester Guildhall). The project of building an all-encompassing college building on Eaton Road, Handbridge, had cost a total of £500,000 and was completed in three phases, which commenced in 1954, 1956 and 1958.